Colonial Women

Niki Walker

Illustrations by Barbara Bedell

🍄 Crabtree Publishing Company

www.crabtreebooks.com

Created by Bobbie Kalman

Dedicated by Niki Walker
To my mom, Liz, for being an amazing woman

Editor-in-Chief
Bobbie Kalman

Author and Editorial director
Niki Walker

Editors
Amanda Bishop
Kathryn Smithyman

Copy editors
Molly Aloian
Rebecca Sjonger

Researcher
Deanna Brady

Art director
Robert MacGregor

Design
Margaret Amy Reiach
Kymberly McKee Murphy

Production coordinator
Heather Fitzpatrick

Photo research
Jaimie Nathan
Laura Hysert

Consultant
Prof. Carol Berkin, Ph.D.,
Department of History, Baruch College, NY

Photographs and reproductions
Claude Moore Colonial Farm: pages 5 (top), 9 (top left, bottom right), 16
Colonial Williamsburg Foundation: title page, pages 5 (bottom), 7,
 9 (top right), 10, 11, 13, 14, 15, 17, 21, 23, 26, 27
Louis Glanzman, National Geographic Society Image Collection: page 30
Historic St. Mary's City/www.stmaryscity.org: page 8
The Metropolitan Museum of Art, The Jules Bache Collection, 1949.
 (49.7.49) Photograph © 1982 The Metropolitan Museum of Art: page 19
Collection of the New-York Historical Society: page 22
Photo courtesy of Old Salem, Winston-Salem, N.C.: pages 3, 6
Parks Canada, Halifax Citadel National Historic Site: page 9 (bottom left)
Réunion des Musées Nationaux/Art Resource, NY: front cover
LaDonna Gulley Warrick: page 31 (top)
Other images by Image Club Graphics

Illustrations
All illustrations by Barbara Bedell except the following:
Margaret Amy Reiach: border (all pages except covers), pages 12,
 18 (bottom), 20, 21, 26, 31 (middle, bottom)

Crabtree Publishing Company
www.crabtreebooks.com   1-800-387-7650

PMB 16A
350 Fifth Avenue
Suite 3308
New York, NY
10118

612 Welland Avenue
St. Catharines
Ontario
Canada
L2M 5V6

73 Lime Walk
Headington
Oxford
OX3 7AD
United Kingdom

Cataloging-in-Publication Data
Walker, Niki
 Colonial women / Niki Walker ; illustrations by Barbara Bedell.
 p. cm. -- (The colonial people series)
Includes index.
Introduces the different skills and often difficult lives of women
on the farm, in business, and on the plantation as the owner's wife
or as a slave in colonial America.
 ISBN 0-7787-0749-0 (RLB) -- ISBN 0-7787-0795-4 (pbk.)
 1. Women--United States--History--Juvenile literature. 2. Women
colonists--United States--Social conditions--Juvenile literature.
3. Women colonists--United States--Social life and customs--
Juvenile literature. 4. United States--History--Colonial period, ca.
1600-1775--Juvenile literature. [1. Women--History--17th century.
2. Women--History--18th century. 3. Colonists. 4. United States--
Social conditions--To 1865. 5. United States--Social life and customs-
-Colonial period, ca. 1600-1775. 6. United States--History--Colonial
period, ca. 1600-1775.] I. Bedell, Barbara, ill. II. Title. III. Series.
 HQ1416 .W35 2003
 305.42'0973--dc21
                                              LC 2002012054

Contents

Colonial women

European **colonists** came to North America in the early 1600s. Most colonists came from towns and cities in Europe, so they were not prepared for the harsh wilderness. There were no farms, roads, or homes. The colonists faced illnesses and food shortages, and many died within a year of arriving.

Going to the New World

The first colonists were men, but women began moving to the **colonies** by the 1620s. Some women traveled with their husbands, but most female settlers made the journey alone, hoping to marry and start a family. Many could only afford the trip from Europe by agreeing to work as **indentured servants**. Their passage was paid for by colonist **sponsors**. Servants repaid their sponsors by working in their homes, fields, or workshops for up to seven years.

Ideas about women

Most colonists believed that men were stronger and smarter than women. They had definite ideas about the roles, jobs, and behaviors that were suitable for women. In general, colonists believed that the role of women was to marry, have children, and run households.

The colonies

When settlers arrived in North America in the early 1600s, they established colonies, which were areas of land that belonged to their kings and queens back in Europe. Many people in Europe were unemployed and did not own any land. They left rented farms and crowded cities in their home countries to claim free land in the colonies. They hoped to begin new lives and perhaps grow wealthy in the New World. Over the years, thousands of Europeans moved to the colonies, and the original Thirteen Colonies, shown right, were formed.

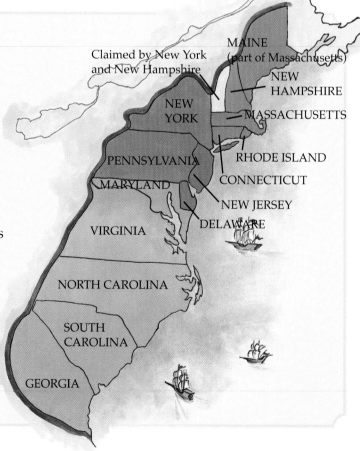

Claimed by New York and New Hampshire

MAINE (part of Massachusetts)

NEW HAMPSHIRE

NEW YORK

MASSACHUSETTS

RHODE ISLAND

PENNSYLVANIA

CONNECTICUT

MARYLAND

NEW JERSEY

DELAWARE

VIRGINIA

NORTH CAROLINA

SOUTH CAROLINA

GEORGIA

Things in common

Women belonged to different **classes**, or levels of society. The wealthiest were part of the highest class, called the **gentry**. Some women were part of the **middling sorts**, or middle class. Members of the **lower sorts**, or lowest class, were **slaves**, servants, and laborers. Despite their class differences, most **colonial** women had several things in common. Since women were not considered equal to men, they could not vote, hold public office, or become religious leaders. They had almost no choices when it came to education or work.

The biggest events in most women's lives were marriage and childbirth.

The lifestyle of a slave, on the right, was different from that of wealthy women.

Other women, other lives

This Moravian woman is preparing flax, the fibers of which can be used to make linen cloth.

Small groups of religious settlers moved to North America from Europe because they were not allowed to practice their religions in their home countries. These colonists formed communities based on their beliefs. The **Puritans** settled in New England and Catholics settled in Maryland, whereas **Moravians**, **Quakers**, and **Mennonites** created settlements in Pennsylvania.

Small communities

Religious communities were close-knit and centered around the church. Most had strict rules about how members should dress and behave. Puritan and Quaker women, for example, were expected to dress plainly and behave modestly. Women who broke the rules were punished. Puritan women obeyed their husbands and ran their homes frugally. Quaker women had a little more freedom. Unlike other colonial women, they could become ministers or church elders. They held monthly meetings to help teach younger women how to become good wives and mothers.

Slave women

During the 1600s, the colonies grew quickly, and there was a lot of work to do. There were not enough indentured servants from Europe to do it all, so colonists started bringing people from Africa to work in the colonies. At first, Africans worked as indentured servants. They were free when their indentures ended. By the end of the 1600s, however, colonists had changed the laws. They brought Africans to the colonies to work as slaves, who had little hope of freedom. Although they lived in the New World, slaves were not considered colonists. Slave women had harsher lives and far fewer rights than European colonial women did. (See pages 14-15.)

Slave women worked long, hard days without pay.

Native American women

Native Americans were already living in North America when the colonists arrived. Native women had well-established roles and customs. In many Eastern Woodland societies, such as the Haudenosaunee (Iroquois) nations, women were farmers and produced the crops that helped feed their families and villages. Men and women shared power in ways that surprised the European colonists. Iroquois women, for example, chose the male leaders of their communities, and they had a strong voice in decisions about war and peace.

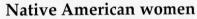

Haudenosaunee women used a mortar and pestle to pound corn into cornmeal for bread or cakes.

A tough new life

Most colonists thought hard physical work, such as clearing land and building homes, was "men's work." There was so much of this work to be done in the colonies, however, that everyone had to help with it, including women. Besides doing their traditional jobs—preparing food, cleaning, caring for children, and treating illnesses—many women worked alongside their husbands and fathers to create new farms and homes for their families. Even after towns and cities were established in the colonies, many women lived rough lives in **rural** areas and on the **frontier**.

Most women grew vegetables to help feed their families. They also grew herbs, which they used to make medicines and to flavor soups and stews.

A day in the life

In the country, a woman usually got up before the rest of her household did—even before the sun came up! Her first chore was to get the fire going. Next, she went to an outdoor well or nearby stream to fetch buckets of water. She then gathered what she needed to prepare breakfast. She milked the cow and collected eggs from the chicken coop. After breakfast was cooked and eaten, the woman began preparing the midday meal, called dinner, which was the main meal of the day. The main dish was often soup or stew, which the woman left to cook over the fire while she began the rest of her chores. Her daily chores may have included washing and mending clothing; drying fruits and vegetables for storage; making jams, pickles, or other **preserves**; baking bread; making candles; tending the vegetable garden and the family's livestock; and helping in the fields. As these pictures show, a woman's work was never done!

A woman cooked meals outdoors or in a fireplace.

Cows had to be milked twice a day.

Women scrubbed and rinsed laundry by hand.

A woman often helped raise crops.

Town and city women

By the end of the 1600s, there were towns and cities throughout the colonies. In these areas, men could work in a trade or profession to support their families. Towns and cities attracted ministers, artisans, tradespeople, and merchants, as well as unskilled workers hoping to find jobs. Married women arrived with their husbands, and single women moved to towns hoping to find work or to marry. Married women often worked in their husbands' shops and taverns, and they also had their jobs to do at home. Unless they had servants or slaves, they still had to cook, clean, and look after their children.

Town and country

The daily lives of women in towns and cities were different from those of women in the country. In towns, women worked with their husbands in businesses rather than on farms. Farmers' wives made much of what their families needed, or they traded with their neighbors. Town women could buy food, cloth, clothing, candles, soap, and almost everything they needed from local shops and markets.

Going out together

In rural areas, women spent most of their time at home. They had few neighbors, and most lived far from one another. Town women had more chances to get out and visit friends. They saw one another when they ran errands and attended church.

Still running the house

A woman who helped her husband in his shop had to run her family's house as well. She prepared the meals, often using food she purchased at the local market. She visited the town's shops and markets a few times a week. She had to know when goods arrived and which shops had just what she wanted. To get everything she needed, the woman often walked from one end of town to the other. It could take half a day to do the shopping! Women learned to bargain for the best prices so that their money would go farther. Some city women also saved money by keeping a small vegetable garden and a cow, pig, or a few chickens in their back yards.

Women often stopped for a chat as they ran their errands in town. Even servants and slaves sometimes found a moment to catch up on news.

Wealthy women often invited guests for tea. Entertaining gave women a chance to stay in touch with others.

11

On a plantation

In the South, many colonists became **plantation** owners. Plantations were farms that specialized in growing one **cash crop**. Cash crops were grown to be sold rather than used by a farmer's family. Plantation owners, or **planters**, sent cash crops such as tobacco, rice, and **indigo**, a plant used to make blue dye, to Europe. Cash crops required a lot of hard work that planters could not do alone. They relied on slaves for the planting, tending, and harvesting of crops.

Throughout the 1600s, most planters lived in small roughly built homes, sometimes with the slaves that worked their fields. Wives often helped their husbands in the fields, while also running a household. In later years, many planters became wealthy enough to build large homes, as shown above. Their wives did not have to spend as much time in the fields.

Even when unexpected guests arrived, a planter's wife offered them a meal and a place to stay.

The wealthy wife

By the mid-1700s, some planters grew wealthy enough to have slaves working in their homes as well as in their fields. **House servants** cleaned the planters' houses and cooked their meals. Even though they had slaves to do the household chores, the wives of planters were kept busy running their homes. They assigned jobs to the servants, checked their work, and planned meals. Wives also supervised their children's lessons, tended to sick slaves, and helped deliver slaves' babies.

Visitors were common on a plantation. A wife was expected to be a good hostess, since her home and hospitality reflected on her husband.

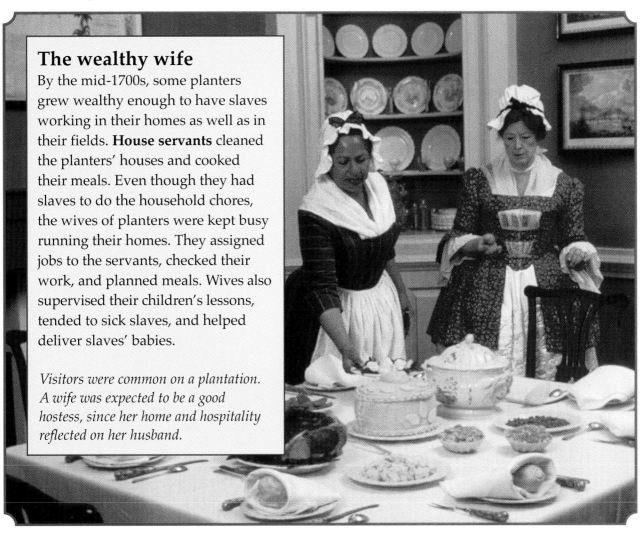

Cut off from the world

Most plantations were so large that neighbors lived many miles apart. Villages, towns, and cities were usually long distances away. Women remained on the plantations while their husbands traveled to town to shop or attend meetings. Visitors were often the only contact women had with the outside world.

One of the responsibilities of a house servant was to help dress the planter's wife in the morning. Garments were often heavy and difficult to fasten.

13

Slave women

Field slaves raised and harvested the crops of their owners and picked bugs off the plants by hand. They worked six days a week from early morning until after sunset.

Most slave women worked on plantations in the South, but some lived in the northern colonies as well. They were considered the property of their owners, as were their children. Slaves were forced to work without pay, and they had no rights or freedom. Some slave women worked as house servants, but most worked as field slaves in rice, indigo, and tobacco fields.

Slave work

House servants did the cooking, cleaning, milking, gardening, and other tasks needed to run a household. In some homes, one servant did all these jobs. Other homes had several servants, each with a specific job to do. Some house servants were cooks; some did the laundry; and others looked after the young children of their owners.

Backbreaking work

Field slaves kept the plantation running. They worked from sunup to sundown six days a week. Their tasks included planting, tending, picking, and packing the crops that their owners sold. Many field slaves died at a young age as a result of their backbreaking labor and long hours in the burning sun.

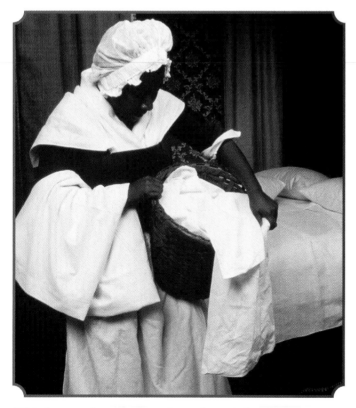

This house slave gathers laundry, makes beds, and cleans the house.

Extra work for extra things

Slaves received basic clothing and a small amount of food from their owners. Some owners allowed and even encouraged their slaves to do additional work in the little spare time they had. Slave women grew vegetable gardens for extra food or did mending or laundry to earn a bit of money.

In the slave quarter

Most slaves lived in small shacks in an area of the plantation called the **slave quarter**. When a slave woman reached the quarter at the end of an exhausting workday, she still could not relax. She had to clean her home, mend torn clothing, prepare the evening meal, and clean up after supper.

A slave and her daughter husk corn they grew in their spare time.

After working in the fields all day and finishing her own chores, a slave woman had only a few moments of leisure time.

*Most girls began learning to knit and sew by the age of four or five. They practiced sewing various stitches on **samplers**.*

Educating girls

Girls were expected to become wives and mothers, so their education taught them the skills they would need to raise children and run households. They learned these skills by spending much of their time working with their mothers. They started helping their mothers at a very young age. Wealthy girls learned how to plan meals, organize and watch over servants, and host parties. Other girls learned to cook, clean, sew, work in the garden, make preserves, and budget money.

Making ladies

Most wealthy colonists sent their sons to boarding schools and hired tutors for their daughters. Some young women learned reading, writing, and arithmetic, but most parents preferred to educate their daughters in music, dance, and entertaining. They felt girls needed to be skilled in these areas to attract "suitable" husbands. Many farming families needed their children to work in the fields, so the children did not have time for school. Mothers usually taught their daughters household skills, whereas fathers taught their sons to farm or practice a trade.

No school for slaves

In many colonies, it was illegal to teach slaves to read and write, but some people did so in secret. Slave mothers also taught their daughters how to sew, cook, and mind their behavior in front of slave owners.

The education of colonial girls was limited, but it was more than that received by girls in much of Europe.

Courtship

Colonial couples did not "date," as people do today. Most young people went through a **courtship**, which was carefully supervised by parents and relatives. Sometimes parents even chose husbands-to-be for their daughters.

Love comes later

Most couples did not get married for love. Women hoped to attract husbands because marriage offered them a home and security. If a young woman also hoped to receive money and support from her family, she had to choose a man who met her parents' approval. A man with power, social status, or money was considered a good match. Parents did not worry if their daughter did not love the man. People believed that love would develop over time.

Courting

People in the lower classes did not have formal courting rituals, but wealthy families did. A wealthy young man was expected to get permission to court a young woman. First, he asked his father and then he approached the woman's father. If both fathers approved, the young man started making formal visits to the young woman's home. He wrote her letters and brought gifts, such as flowers, as well.

For love or money?

A girl's father was expected to offer a **dowry**, or marriage gift, for his daughter. Dowries could include money, livestock, furniture, and even slaves. A girl with a large dowry had a much better chance of finding a husband of status than a girl without a dowry. Girls who were less wealthy often married farmers or tradesmen. These men wanted wives who were able to work hard, run a household, and be frugal with money.

It's official!

Before couples could marry, they posted **banns**, or wedding announcements, in a public place such as a church. The banns gave others in the community a chance to protest the marriage. It also ensured that young men and women did not marry without the approval of their parents. Parents could not withhold their approval without a good reason, however. Some young colonists sued their parents for preventing marriages without good cause.

The young woman on the right has received flowers and a note from her suitor.

Wedding bells

Different types of weddings took place in the various colonies. The wealthy couple above was married in a church, but most wedding ceremonies were held in a bride's home. Families and friends gathered to watch the couple exchange their vows. In northern colonies, ceremonies were simple, and weddings were followed by a meal. In the South, wedding guests enjoyed several days of feasting and dancing. Not all weddings involved a ceremony. In some areas, a couple was considered married if the man asked the woman and she said yes!

Covered up

As soon as a woman married, she was **covered** by her husband, which meant that she was no longer an individual person. She could not own a business or any property, keep the wages she earned, or sign contracts. Unless the couple signed a special contract, any property the woman owned before marriage became her husband's. By law, she did not even own her clothes!

Why get married?

Although unmarried women had more freedom than married women did, very few girls wanted to remain single. Unmarried women past the age of twenty-five were seen as hopeless "old maids." People believed marriage was a woman's reason for living, so an unmarried woman was often pitied and distrusted by her neighbors. Unmarried women lived with married relatives. They were expected to work hard and had almost no say in the household.

Free again

A **widow**, or woman whose husband died, enjoyed more freedom than a married woman did. As a widow, she became an individual person again, which meant she could own property and sign contracts. She was entitled to one-third of her husband's property, and she could take over his business. She often managed the entire **estate** until her children became old enough to inherit their shares.

Slave weddings

Although slave marriages were not considered legal, many slaves did marry. The ceremonies were performed by a respected older slave, the slave owner, or a local minister. Some weddings were held in the slave owner's house, whereas others were held outdoors. Many couples added "jumping the broom" to their wedding ceremonies. In this tradition, the husband and wife jumped over a sage-grass broom that was laid on the ground. It was said that the person who jumped farthest would have the most influence in the marriage!

Some slaves saw jumping the broom as making the leap into married life.

Family life

In colonial times, most people believed that **patriarchal** families were best. In a patriarchal family, the father was the head of the household. He controlled the family's money and decided on rules and punishments. His wife was supposed to obey his decisions on all matters. Her rank was lower than his in the household but higher than that of the children, servants, and other relatives who lived in the home. Although people liked the idea of patriarchal families, many families did not actually live this way. Wives often voiced their opinions and worked as their husbands' partners.

Many women chose to remarry after their husbands died. Their families were made up of step-parents, step-siblings, and half-siblings, just as many families are today.

Motherhood

Most colonial women had several children, and many had their first baby before the age of twenty. After that, women usually gave birth to another baby every year or two. When women gave birth, their female friends and relatives gathered to help them. **Midwives** delivered the babies because people felt it was improper for male doctors to do so.

The dangers of childbirth

Many women died while giving birth or shortly after. Most were tired and weak from hard work, and they were not strong enough to survive the births of their fourth or fifth babies.

Colonial childhood

Being a child in a colonial family was quite different from being a child today. People knew little about germs and illness, so many babies got sick and died before their first birthdays. Children who survived often had to care for their younger siblings, as well as doing other chores around the house, farm, or business. By the time children were five years old, they were expected to earn their keep. There was little time for games or play. Many parents were stern with their children, demanding obedience and respect. In later years, parents became more affectionate with their children.

Stealing away
Unhappy couples could not divorce, but they could separate. When couples split, wives were often left with nothing. Rather than waiting for a formal separation, many wives sneaked away from their homes at night with whatever they could carry.

Slave families
Slaves could be sold or traded at any time, but some owners tried to keep slave families together. When these owners died or had debts, however, families were often split up to be sold. Sometimes family members were sent to distant plantations and never saw one another again. Some owners punished slaves by selling them or their family members. For many slaves, "family" came to include good friends and other people they loved.

Jobs for women

Today, many people are surprised to learn that colonial women worked outside the home. In fact, many women had jobs besides their duties as housewives. Some women worked at trades or in shops, helping their husbands or fathers. Some made handicrafts that they sold or traded in order to buy extra things for their families. Unmarried women often worked as servants, teachers, **mantua makers**, laundresses, farm help, and midwives. Midwives earned a living by helping women with childbirth.

Working for themselves

A few businesses were almost always owned by unmarried women. A **milliner** shop sold stylish goods that were **imported** from Europe. Mantua makers sewed fashionable gowns for women. Many wigmakers were women, as well. They used human, goat, horse, and yak hair to weave wigs, which were worn by most men in colonial times. Wigmakers also cleaned and cared for men's wigs and styled women's hair.

Working at home

Many women made foods such as butter, pies, jams, and pickles to sell to local merchants. Some made goods such as baskets or candles. Women also earned money by spinning yarn and thread or weaving cloth. They sold these goods to tailors and milliners. Women could also take in laundry and mend people's clothes as other ways of earning extra money.

Medical workers

Some women worked in **apothecary** shops, which were like colonial drug stores. The women ground herbs and other ingredients and mixed **poultices**, or treatments for infections. A few women earned money as healers. They did not have formal training, but they were known for their healing abilities. These women could charge money for doing what most women did for free as wives and mothers.

Entertainers

Colonists usually made their own entertainment, but some cities and towns had theaters or taverns that attracted professional singers and musicians. Although most entertainers were male, a few were women.

Widows' work

Many working women were widows. Wives of tradesmen often took over their husbands' businesses after their husbands died. These women worked at jobs that were considered men's work. They became innkeepers, tavern keepers, printers, merchants, and craftspeople such as blacksmiths, shipbuilders, and silversmiths.

Games and pastimes

Both girls and boys enjoyed playing marble games. This game was called Ring Taw.

People made up games using items they had around the house, such as lengths of rope.

Colonial women worked hard, so free time was a luxury for most. Wealthy women had more leisure time than others had, since servants did their cooking, cleaning, and laundry. Women and girls of all classes did, however, find ways to take a break from the grind of their daily work and have some fun. They enjoyed pastimes such as card games, playing musical instruments, and going horseback riding.

Farm fun

Farm women often found ways to make big chores fun. They held work parties called **bees** to help one another with jobs such as sewing, making quilts, harvesting crops, and husking corn. When there was a big social event, such as a wedding or barn-raising, women helped one another prepare food for the party.

Toys for girls

Most of the toys that were imported from Europe were very expensive. Wealthy parents bought porcelain dolls and other imported toys for their daughters, but most girls played with homemade toys. Girls made dolls from leftover corn husks or scraps of fabric, used ordinary rope for skipping games, and rolled old hoops in races.

Gathering with friends

Most slaves did not work on Sundays. On Saturday nights, they often had outdoor parties in the slave quarter of a plantation, as shown above. They sang songs, danced together, told stories, and played homemade drums and instruments made from dried gourds. They also attended religious services in the evenings and on Sundays. In some areas, slaves were not allowed to gather and had to meet in secret.

Women's clothing

A woman's clothing often reflected her class. For example, wealthy women wore fine garments to show that they could afford expensive things. Women of the lower sorts wore clothing that allowed them to move easily while working. Despite these differences, all women wore similar under-garments, over which they layered skirts or dresses. Skirts were always long, and sleeves always covered the elbows.

Girls and women always wore loose linen or cotton dresses, called **shifts**, *underneath their clothing.*

Most women laced **stays** *over their shifts to give their torsos a fashionable cone shape. Stays were stiffened with strips of metal, wood, or whalebone to help improve posture.*

Skirts did not have sewn-in pockets. Women tied pockets around their waists, under their skirts.

Women wore knit stockings made of cotton or silk. Most stockings were white, but some had fancy designs stitched near the ankle.

Many women wore wooden or metal frames, called **hoops,** *to fill out their skirts. They wore hoops for events such as balls or dinner parties.*

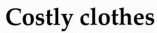

Costly clothes

Wealthy, fashionable women wore fancy dresses, known as **gowns**, which had fitted **bodices** with floor-length skirts attached. Gowns were made of expensive fabrics such as fine silk or embroidered cotton.

When going out, most men and some women wore wigs. For special occasions, women had their hair done in fancy styles. Sometimes they powdered their hair.

Wide skirts were fashionable. Women wore hoops to make their skirts look fuller.

*Women wore their hair in coiled braids or buns. At home, they covered their hair with **mobcaps** made of linen or cotton.*

Working clothes

Women who worked at home or in shops wore simpler outfits than those worn by wealthy women. Their gowns were made of plain cotton, wool, or linen fabric. Instead of a gown, some women wore calf-length petticoats with jackets, which allowed them to move more easily. Slaves and women who worked outdoors wore plain, loose blouses with their petticoats. These shirts were easier to sew than bodices or jackets, and they were much cooler.

Some women wore jackets instead of bodices.

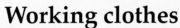

29

Notable colonial women

Colonial women were expected to keep their place in society, but several female colonists chose to defy their traditional roles. These women became famous for their achievements. Some, such as Eliza Pinckney, are known for their success in business. Pinckney not only ran successful plantations while raising her family, but she also invented a way to make blocks of blue dye from indigo plants. Her invention helped make South Carolina's economy stronger, as indigo plantations thrived. Deborah Moody was another woman who stood out in colonial times. She was the first woman to vote in a colonial election. These pages highlight some other famous female colonists.

Margaret Brent

Margaret Brent came to the colonies in 1638 and received a land grant from the Governor of Maryland. Brent became the first female lawyer in the colonies. She represented her brothers and various women at different times in front of the courts. When the governor died, she was left in charge of running his estate and paying his many debts. More than once, Brent tried to gain the right to vote. She was never allowed to vote, even though she owned land and had experience with law and politics. She died on her plantation in Virginia in 1671. She never married.

Anne Bradstreet

Born in 1612, Anne Bradstreet was a Puritan poet. In her time, women writers were looked down upon by society. Bradstreet wrote poems for her own enjoyment. Without her knowledge, however, a relative sneaked a copy of the poems to England, where they were published in 1650. The book was a first in many ways: it was the first book published by a North American, by a woman, and by a Puritan.

© LaDonna Gulley Warrick

Anne Hutchinson

Anne Hutchinson, a Puritan, was born in England in 1590. She came to the colonies in 1634 and settled in Boston. Hutchinson quickly made a name for herself among other Puritans by hosting weekly meetings for women at her house. She gave the women an opportunity to voice opinions and discuss religious ideas. Hutchinson gained a following as she began to speak out against the clergy and their method of preaching. Many people, including several prominent men, agreed with her views. The religious leaders had the support of political leaders, however. In 1637, they put Hutchinson on trial. She was found guilty of **heresy** and banished from Boston.

Phillis Wheatley

Phillis Wheatley was born in Senegal in 1753. She was kidnapped and then sold as a slave in Massachusetts to John Wheatley, whose wife taught her to read and write English, Greek, and Latin. Wheatley's first poem was published in 1767 and, in 1773, a book of her poetry was published in England. She was the first African poet in the colonies to have her poems published.

Glossary

Note: Boldfaced words that are defined in the book may not appear in the glossary.

apothecary One who prepares, prescribes, and sells medicines in a shop

bodice The fitted part of a dress that covers from the shoulders to the waist

class A division in a community based on wealth and social standing

colonial Relating to living in a colony or to the period when European countries ruled North America

colonist A person who lived in one of the colonies in North America

colony An area ruled by a faraway country

courtship The time before marriage when a man is trying to win the affection of a woman

estate A person's property and possessions

frontier An area of unsettled land just beyond or at the edge of a settled area

heresy An opinion that does not agree with established religious beliefs

imported Describing items brought from foreign places

indentured servant A person who has promised services to another for a specified amount of time

Mennonite A member of the Anabaptist church who lives a simple life

midwife A woman who is trained to help women give birth

Moravian A member of a Protestant group founded in eastern Europe in the 1400s

preserves Fruit cooked in sugar and sealed in a jar to prevent it from spoiling

Puritan A Protestant in the 1500s and 1600s who believed in strict discipline and a simple religious life

plantation A large farm where one main crop, such as tobacco or rice, is grown

Quaker A member of the Society of Friends

rural Describing areas in the country

sampler A decorative piece of cloth embroidered with designs or letters

slave A person treated as property and forced to work for no pay

sponsor A person who paid the fare for another person to travel to North America

Index

1 2 3 4 5 6 7 8 9 0   Printed in the U.S.A.   2 1 0 9 8 7 6 5 4 3